Vroom!
Lamborghini

by Mari Schuh

Ideas for Parents and Teachers

Bullfrog Books let children practice reading informational text at the earliest reading levels. Repetition, familiar words, and photo labels support early readers.

Before Reading

- Discuss the cover photo. What does it tell them?

- Look at the picture glossary together. Read and discuss the words.

During Reading

- "Walk" through the book with the reader. Discuss new or unfamiliar words. Sound them out together.

- Look at the photos together. Point out the photo labels.

After Reading

- Prompt the child to think more. Ask: Have you seen a Lamborghini? What color was it?

Bullfrog Books are published by Jump!
3500 American Blvd W, Suite 150
Bloomington, MN 55431
www.jumplibrary.com

Copyright © 2026 Jump! International copyright reserved in all countries. No part of this book may be reproduced in any form without written permission from the publisher.

Jump! is a division of FlutterBee Education Group.

Library of Congress Cataloging-in-Publication Data

Names: Schuh, Mari C., 1975– author.
Title: Lamborghini / by Mari Schuh.
Description: Minneapolis, MN: Jump!, Inc., [2026]
Series: Vroom! | Includes index.
Audience: Ages 5–8
Identifiers: LCCN 2024058230 (print)
LCCN 2024058231 (ebook)
ISBN 9798896620235 (hardcover)
ISBN 9798896620242 (paperback)
ISBN 9798896620259 (ebook)
Subjects: LCSH: Lamborghini automobile—Juvenile literature.
Classification: LCC TL215.L33 S358 2026 (print)
LCC TL215.L33 (ebook)
DDC 629.222/2–dc23/eng/20250208
LC record available at https://lccn.loc.gov/2024058230
LC ebook record available at https://lccn.loc.gov/2024058231

Editor: Jenna Gleisner
Designer: Anna Peterson

Photo Credits: Grzegorz Czapski/Shutterstock, cover; Maksim Denisenko/Shutterstock, 1; Mike Mareen/Shutterstock, 3; Alexandre Prevot/Shutterstock, 4, 5, 20–21; Christopher Lyzcen/Shutterstock, 6–7, 23tm; Marko583/Dreamstime, 9; Max Earey/Dreamstime, 10–11, 23tl; PuccaPhotography/Shutterstock, 12–13; Fabio Pagani/Dreamstime, 14–15, 23tr; Wirestock Creators/Shutterstock, 16 (foreground); mares90/Shutterstock, 16 (background); Wirestock/Dreamstime, 17, 23bl; Bruno Coelho/Dreamstime, 18–19, 23bm; Dong liu/Shutterstock, 22; Mark Castiglia/Dreamstime, 23br; PhatTai/Shutterstock, 24.

Printed in the United States of America at Corporate Graphics in North Mankato, Minnesota.

Table of Contents

Low Cars	4
Parts of a Lamborghini	22
Picture Glossary	23
Index	24
To Learn More	24

Lamborghini (lam-ber-GEE-nee)

Low Cars

This car is low to the ground.

It is a Lamborghini!

We call it a Lambo.

The **logo** is black.

It has a gold bull.

The first one was made in 1964.

Wow!

Lambos have sharp **edges**.
They come in bright colors.

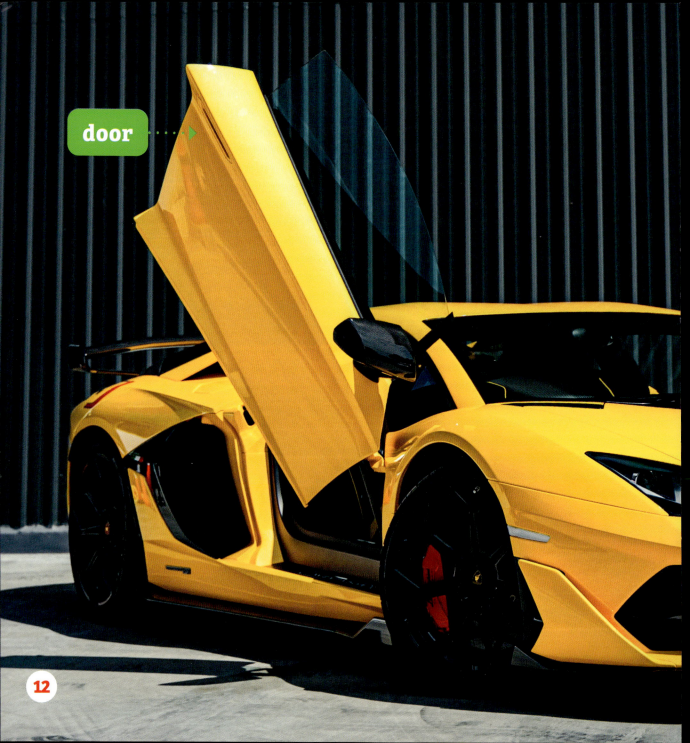

These cars have scissor doors.

They swing up.

Fun!

There are different **models**.

This one is a race car.

It zooms around a **track**!

The Huracán is popular. See it go!

The Urus is an **SUV**.

Look at the Aventador.
The roof is down.
Feel the wind!

Parts of a Lamborghini

A Lamborghini Veneno can go 221 miles (356 kilometers) per hour! Take a look at the parts of a Lamborghini!

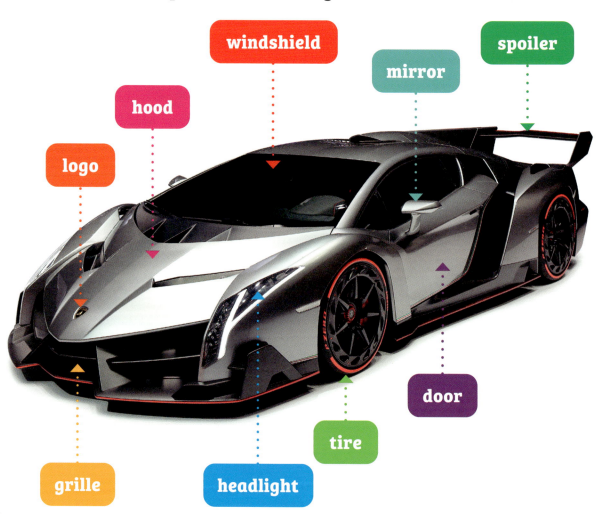

22

Picture Glossary

edges
The ends or points where an object ends.

logo
A symbol that stands for a company.

models
Particular types or designs.

spoiler
A wing-shaped part on a car.

SUV
Short for Sport Utility Vehicle. A car that can drive where there are no roads.

track
A path or course made for race cars. Many tracks are oval.

Index

Aventador 20
colors 10
doors 13
edges 10
Huracán 16
Italy 8
logo 7
models 14
race car 14
spoiler 17
SUV 19
Urus 19

To Learn More

Finding more information is as easy as 1, 2, 3.

❶ Go to **www.factsurfer.com**

❷ Enter **"Lamborghini"** into the search box.

❸ Choose your book to see a list of websites.